PARENT HANDBOOK ON GETTING CHILDREN READY FOR LEARNING

by

Dr. Barbara Holmes

Dr. Angela Seay

Avid Readers Publishing Group
Lakewood, California

Parent Handbook on Getting Children Ready for Learning

i

Avid Readers Publishing Group

http://www.avidreaderspg.com

ISBN-13: 978-1-935105-55-8

Printed in the United States

Table of Contents

Introduction	1
What Parents Do Matters	4
What Parents Say Matters	5
Holmes/Seay Word List	6
Improving Your Child's Language Abilities	7
Get Your Child a Library Card	9
Strategies to Enhance Language Abilities	10
Start Your CHILD File	13
Good Parenting Behaviors	14
Ten Basic Principles of Good Parenting	16
Changing Your Child's Behavior	20
Practices to Avoid Parenting in Anger	23
Parents' Checklist for Choosing Child Care	24
Parenting Checklist	26
Kindergarten Readiness Checklist	29
References	30

About the Authors

Dr. Barbara Holmes has thirty-six years of education experience and has successfully raised two high achieving children. Dr. Holmes earned the PhD from the University of Connecticut, Masters Degree in Educational Administration and Supervision and Bachelor's Degree in Speech and English from Stetson University. Dr. Holmes has been honored as a Distinguished Graduate of the University of Connecticut and was bestowed the Honorary Doctor of Laws from Stetson University. She is the recipient of the Mary McLeod Bethune Award from the National Council of Negro Women and a lifelong member of Alpha Kappa Alpha Sorority. Dr. Holmes is a published scholar and currently serves as Chief Executive Officer for Virtual Learning Associates, Atlanta, GA.

Dr. Angela Seay has fifteen years of K-12 teaching and administrative experience and ten years as an Educational Consultant. She has an earned EdD in Instructional Leadership and EdS in Curriculum and Instruction. Dr. Seay also earned the MEd in Administration and Supervision from the University of West Alabama, and a BS in Early Childhood Education from Concordia University. Dr. Seay is a published author and currently serves as Chief Executive Officcer for Everybody Seay Read and Education Coordinator for HeadStart.

Introduction

"Thirty years of research tells us that the starting point of American education is parent expectations and parental involvement with their children's education."

– U.S. Department of Education, 1994

Parents are a child's first and most influential teachers. Parents play a major role in encouraging and supporting learning at home. Parents teach children how to communicate and how to relate to significant others in the child's circle of influence. When parents receive good information and are taught what to do in helping their children learn, the impact of this positive regard and support for the development of the child is carried over into the school setting. This book is dedicated to parents in recognition of the critical role they play in nurturing and supporting learning in the home environment.

Through this handbook, we intend to work with parents in sharing knowledge about what the research says about getting young children ready for learning. The resources in this handbook have been assembled as a handy reference for parents. We appreciate all of the researchers whose work is included.

Children learn what they live! 

"You must be the change you wish to see."

– Mahatma Gandhi

Parental love, support and positive regard are core essential habits that every parent should embrace. Children who live in a loving, caring environment learn how to demonstrate these traits to others. They learn how to play well and exhibit caring behaviors toward other children. They are also able to be respectful of persons in authority because they have been taught this respect for others at home.

When parents invest love into a child, this is a lifelong gift that supports the child's develoment in every way. Loved children are happy, confident and positive because parents have taught them that they are important and valued persons. Parents can show their love by showing affection towards the child, hugging the child, showering the child with positive praise and of course, providing quality care.

Parents, your job is so very important and taking the time to do it provides lifelong benefits to your child.

"We must do the things we think we cannot do. The future belongs to those who believe in the beauty of their dreams."
— Eleanor Roosevelt.

Parents, the power of your beliefs in the potential of the child propels the child toward successful outcomes. Children need to know that you believe they can succeed; that you believe they have potential; that you believe that they are worthy, valuable human beings; that you believe they can learn, and that you believe they will have a positive and powerful future.

Tell your children daily how much you believe in them, love them and how very special they are. Catch your child doing something good and celebrate this small success. Watch your child smile and beam in the presence of your praise. Parents, you have the power to transform and shape the life of your child. Use this power wisely!

What PARENTS Do Matters

"While we try to teach our children all about life, our children teach us what life is all about."
-Angela Schwindt

Azar (2000) reported that in a study that targeted parents whose children were about to enter school, it was found that improving parenting practices had a significant effect one, two and then four years later on children's behavior and success in schools. Consequently, it is important that parents be involved with their children and demonstrate good parenting practices that lead to positive developmental growth of the child.

Start active parenting in the early years. Research from Kansas researchers on early development shows us how infants can make fine auditory and visual discriminations in the very first months of life. Babies know and can recognize their parents' voices. Talk to your child. Sing to your child. Embrace your child in the world of language.

All children acquire their language skills from the language used in the home environment. The home and family environment and the child's family provide the vast learning laboratory for the acquisition of language, culture and communication. We all know that experience is cumulative. Therefore, the amount of talking and singing used by families adds up to tremendous differences in a child's cumulative experience with language development.

What PARENTS Say Matters

"There are two lasting bequests we can give our children. One is roots. The other is wings."

-Hodding Carter, Jr.

Stephens (2004) advises parents to be good role models for their children. Stephens says that children respect adults and family members who "Walk their talk." Children are sensitive and very perceptive in determining what is authentic and what is not in terms of how they are treated. Adults who are credible mean what they say and say what they mean.

In this regard, parents need to be ever mindful of what they are saying around children. Children will learn their language skills from you and will use this language in the same way that you do. Even babies will react to your words, tone, delivery, volume and sincerity. The things that parents say to children are critically important.

In the early years, children will need to acquire a vocabulary with which to negotiate their world. Pay attention to the words your child is learning and help your child acquire a rich vocabulary which will be needed for later reading skills. While most parents are excited by a child's first words, there needs to be excitement about all of the other words the child learns to use as well.

To support communication growth of the child, the authors have developed a word list for those children getting ready for preschool.

Holmes/Seay Word List

Note to Parents: Children are more highly verbal today and are growing up in a technology- rich learning environment. The following word list was developed to help you become aware of the words that children frequently hear in the preschool years as you work to help develop their vocabulary.

a	and	apple	ball	big	bat	bath	bird	black	cat
arm	leg	foot	finger	eye	ear	face	hand	neck	fat
chair	door	come	sit	me	mine	yours	my	mat	look
up	down	play	friend	toy	run	we	jump	stand	read
red	blue	yellow	white	green	brown	one	two	three	four
five	six	seven	eight	nine	ten	milk	water	cereal	bread
love	hug	kiss	wait	go	sing	walk	talk	see	mother
father	house	car	TV	pen	paper	help	work	eat	sleep
small	round	sky	rain	bag	shoe	story	scissors	circle	name
dog	tree	table	socks	back	shirt	cup	pencil	book	phone

Improving Your Child's Language Abilities: What You Can Do

- Sing to your child

  Hearing the sound of your voice is very comforting and soothing to your child, this is why lullabies are so important.

- Talk to your kids

  Talk in complete sentences. Describe the world around you. And what is going on in the family. Tell the child how much she/he is loved.

- Tell your kids about things in the home

  Talk to your child about the furnishings in the home. Make sure your child knows terms like "bed", "toilet", "chair", "table", "refrigerator", "stove", "sofa", "desk", "rug"

- Listen to your kids

  Listen to what your child has to say; Engage your child in conversation; ask additional questions to keep the child talking; Show excitement about the subject of the discussion.

▪ Help your child make choices

Help your child make choices that they care about. For example, "Would you like eggs or cereal for breakfast?", "Do you want to wear the red socks or the blue socks?", "Do you want to read your favorite book?"

Get Your Child a Library Card

The Baltimore County Public Schools has a great model program called "My First Library Card". A description of the program is below. Check with your local community library and see if a similar program exists.

My First Library Card

The My First Library Card program provides library cards for children ages birth through kindergarten in all library branches, and through cooperation with various pre-school programs and Baltimore County Public Schools.

Here's why a library card is a great thing for your child: Using library materials helps children learn to read well. Good readers are better students. Children who read well grow up to be active and successful adults.

What strategies based on scientifically-based reading research, can you use to enhance the language, cognitive, and early reading development of preschool age children?

Research shows that the following strategies and activities are effective in developing the language, cognitive, and early reading skills of young children:

⇒ *A high-quality oral language and literacy-rich environment.* A high-quality oral language environment includes adults reading books aloud to children, asking children, for example, to predict what might happen next in the book, and asking children predictive and analytic questions that help them analyze the story. Adults use rich and varied vocabulary and provide children frequent opportunities during all activities to ask and answer questions. Teachers engage children in conversation and use linguistic awareness games, such as songs and nursery rhymes, and rhythmic activities that are focused on phonological awareness to help develop children's oral language skills.

UNITED STATES DEPARTMENT OF EDUCATION (2007)

What can you as a PARENT do?

"Listening is a high art of loving. Ask yourself, "When was the last time I really listened to my child? When someone is ready to share, three magic words amplify your connection, and they are: 'Tell me more.'" -Rev. Mary Manin Morrissey

- It's never too early to read to your baby. Try rhymes like "Mary Had a Little Lamb", a birthday card, a cereal box, even the newspaper! The sounds children hear are what matter.

- Keep a book in your diaper bag. You value reading, and carrying a book with you shows it!

- Introduce simple pictures and storybooks as your baby grows. Shapes, Colors and sounds will delight. Try picture books for songs that you can sing together.

- Change your voice for different characters in a book. Help your child learn the characters through your voice.

- Point out people and objects. Ask your child, "Where is the dog hiding?" or other questions about the book before or after you read the page.

- Read the same book over and over -- really. It helps children feel secure.

- Discuss the stories you are reading with your child. Ask questions such as "What sound will the dog make?"

- Discuss the parts of the book. What is the front of the

book? Where does the story start? Who is the author? As you read, move your finger to show how the words move across the page.

- Visit the library often. And let children help select their own books.

- Make a special time for reading aloud -- after dinner, before bed ... anytime. Talk calmly and take your time, let your child know this is important to you.

- Let your children see you reading. They want to imitate you. Talk about what you read.

Get your child a library card today!

Endorsed by:

James T. Smith, Jr., Baltimore County Executive

Baltimore County Public Schools

Baltimore County Local Management Board

Start Your CHILD File

In addition to the Library Card, parents need to organize a records file of important documents that will be needed for school-
ing. Start gathering the following:

- **Birth Certificate**

- **Immunization Record**

- **Pediatrician Records**

- **Dental Records**

- **Vision Records**

- **Proof of Residency**

Keep these documents handy in a secure place so that they are
easily retrievable when you need them.

Good Parenting Behaviors

"**Good parenting includes the ability to identify and understand what a child needs. When appropriate, these parents will separate what the child's needs are from their own needs and can place the needs of their child before their own.**"

By: Michael G. Conner, Psy.D
http://www.crisiscounseling.com/Articles/GoodParenting.htm

Schutz and colleagues (1989) suggest a group of parenting behaviors that are widely accepted by family experts as the means for parents to support the development of competent children.

Good Parenting Behaviors

- Parent is actively and positively involved in child's life.

- There are direct, open, and cooperative dialogues between parent and child.

- Parent cooperatively communicates with other parent.

- Parent is flexible in behavior and limit setting.

- Parent appropriately modulates expressions of love and intimacy.

- Parent sets clear boundaries between child and environment.

- Parent identifies and understands child's needs.

- Parent accurately observes child's behavior and own behavior.

- Parent develops and nurtures independence, individuation, social responsibility, and self-confidence.

- Parent develops and nurtures child's self-esteem.

- Parent is knowledgeable about child's strengths and weaknesses.

- Parent is perceived as a positive role model.

- Parent applies appropriate discipline.

- Parent supports child's relationship with other parent.

- Parent encourages socially appropriate behaviors and respect for rules governing society.

"Children are the keys of paradise" -Richard Stoddard

Ten Basic Principles of Good Parenting

1. What you do matters.

"Tell yourself that every day that how you treat and respond to your child should come from a knowledgeable, deliberate sense of what you want to accomplish. Always ask yourself: What effect will my decision have on my child?"

2. You cannot be too loving.

"When it comes to genuine expressions of warmth and affection, you cannot love your child too much. It is simply not possible to spoil a child with love. What we often think of as the product of spoiling a child is never the result of showing a child too much love. It is usually the consequence of giving a child things in place of love—things like leniency, lowered expectations or material possessions."

3. Be involved in your child's life.

"Being an involved parent takes time and is hard work, and it often means rethinking and rearranging your priorities. It frequently means sacrificing what you want to do for what your child needs you to do. Be there mentally as well as physically."

4. Adapt your parenting to fit your child.

"Make sure your parenting keeps pace with your child's development. You may wish you could slow down or freeze-frame your child's life, but this is the last thing he wants. You may be fighting getting older, but all he wants is to grow up. The same drive for independence that is making your three-year-old say 'no' all the time is what's motivating him to be toilet trained. The same intellectual growth spurt that is making your 13-year-old curious and inquisitive in the classroom also is making her argumentative at the dinner table."

5. Establish and set rules.

"If you don't manage your child's behavior when he is young, he will have a hard time learning how to manage himself when he is older and you aren't around. Any time of the day or night, you should always be able to answer these three questions: Where is my child? Who is with my child? What is my child doing? The rules your child has learned from you are going to shape the rules he applies to himself."

6. Foster your child's independence.

"Setting limits helps your child develop a sense of self-control. Encouraging independence helps her develop a sense of self-direction. To be successful in life, she's going to need both. Accepting that it is normal for children to push for autonomy is absolutely key to effective parenting. Many parents mistakenly equate their child's independence with rebelliousness or disobedience. Children push for independence because it is part of human nature to want to feel in control rather than to feel controlled by someone else."

7. Be consistent.

"If your rules vary from day to day in an unpredictable fashion, or if you enforce them only intermittently, your child's misbehavior is your fault, not his. Your most important disciplinary tool is consistency. Identify your non-negotiables. The more your authority is based on wisdom and not on power, the less your child will challenge it."

8. Avoid harsh discipline.

"Of all the forms of punishment that parents use, the one with the worst side effects is physical punishment. Children who are spanked, hit or slapped are more prone to fighting with other children. They are more likely to be bullies and more likely to use aggression to solve disputes with others."

9. Explain your rules and decisions.

"Good parents have expectations they want their child to live up to. Generally, parents overexplain to young children and underexplain to adolescents. What is obvious to you may not be evident to a 12-year-old. He doesn't have the priorities, judgment or experience that you have."

10. Treat your child with respect.

"The best way to get respectful treatment from your child is to treat him respectfully. You should give your child the same courtesies you would give to anyone else. Speak to him politely. Respect his opinion. Pay attention when he is speaking to you. Treat him kindly. Try to please him when you can. Children treat others the way their parents treat them. Your relationship with your child is the foundation for her relationships with others."
http://www.chiff.com/a/good-parenting.htm

Journal of the American Academy of Pediatrics

CONCLUSIONS:

A dearth of positive **parenting behaviors** plus negative perceptions of children, with or without psychosocial risk factors, negatively affect child development, which is apparent as early as 6 months of age. The older the child is, the greater the performance gaps are. Language development is particularly at risk when **parenting** is problematic. Findings underscore the importance of early development promotion with parents, focusing on their talking, playing, and reading with children, and the need for interventions regarding psychosocial risk factors. PEDIATRICS Vol. 125 No. 2 February 2010, pp. 313-319 (doi:10.1542/peds.2008-3129

Child Behavior: What Parents Can Do to Change Their Child's Behavior

"Let parents bequeath to their children not riches, but the spirit of reverence." -Plato

What are some good ways to reward my child?

Beat the Clock (good method for a dawdling child)

Ask the child to do a task. Set a timer. If the task is done before the timer rings, your child gets a reward. To decide the amount of time to give the child, figure out your child's "best time" to do that task and add 5 minutes.

The Good Behavior Game (good for teaching a new behavior)

Write a short list of good behaviors on a chart and mark the chart with a star each time you see the good behavior. After your child has earned a small number of stars (depending on the child's age), give him or her a reward.

Good Marks/Bad Marks (best method for difficult, highly active children)

In a short time (about an hour) put a mark on a chart or on your child's hand each time you see him or her performing a good behavior. For example, if you see your child playing quietly, solving a problem without fighting, picking up toys or reading a book, you would mark the chart. After a certain number of marks, give your child a reward. You can also make negative marks each time a bad behavior occurs. If you do this, only give your child a reward if there are more positive marks than negative marks.

Developing Quiet Time (often useful when you're making supper).

Ask your child to play quietly alone or with a sibling for a short time (maybe 30 minutes). Check on your child frequently (every 2 to 5 minutes, depending on the child's age) and give a reward or a token for each few minutes they were quiet or playing well. Gradually increase the intervals (go from checking your child's behavior every 2 to 5 minutes to checking every 30 minutes), but continue to give rewards for each time period your child was quiet or played well.

http://familydoctor.org/online/famdocen/home/children/parents/behavior/201.html

Dr. William Sears coined the term "attachment parenting" in the 1970s. He observed mothers in other cultures nurturing their babies similar to how they would of thousands of years ago. From that, he theorized that there were eight ideals of parenting that were especially effective in promoting a healthy, loving relationship between parent and child. The eight ideals are:

- Being prepared for childbirth

- Being emotionally responsive to your baby's needs

- Breastfeeding - Wearing your baby (in a sling or carrier)

- Co-sleeping (sleeping with your baby)

- Avoiding separation from your baby

- Positive discipline (avoiding spanking, yelling, etc.)

- Maintaining balance in family life

  http://www.kidschecklist.com/parenting.html

10 Practices to Avoid Parenting in Anger

1) Avoid immediately lashing out in anger. This only produces negative results.

2) Avoid personalizing a younger child's misbehavior or crying as an offense against you. Personalizing will cause you to be angry and aggressive.

3) If needed, briefly separate yourself from your child until your anger subsides.

4) Think through times when you are most likely to become angry with your child. Prepare yourself for these situations. In your own mind, create some ways in which you will deal with that situation the next time it arises.

5) If possible, try to avoid disciplining your child in public view.

6) When you do fail in anger, apologize to your child. Saying you are sorry has much restoring power.

7) Focus on what is right and best for the child, not what feels right or best.

8) Take a break from your child when stress builds up over time. Find a safe friend or family member who can watch your child for a reasonable time period.

9) Seek professional counseling if your anger is becoming a problem or your child's misbehavior seems abnormal.

10). **Count to Ten and Cool Down!**

A helpful tool to avoid having an outburst toward your child is to pause before your outburst and count to ten. This gives you valuable time to cool down in order to avoid a harmful reaction.

1. Pause before you burst out in anger
2. Count to Ten: 1 2 3 4 5 6 7 8 9 10
3. Move beyond a harmful reaction to a helpful response

PARENTS' Checklist for Choosing Child Care

In order to better serve parents, the Office of Inspector General's Division of Regulated Child Care has developed a short checklist to help parents evaluate the child care center you are considering. Remember the 3 P's-Paperwork-Premises-Programming.

- **Paperwork**

  - ☐ Is a license posted? All child care providers must have a valid license.
  - ☐ Did you look at the compliance reports completed by OIG that are posted?
  - ☐ Did you look at the daily schedule to see what children are learning and what the activities are for the day?
  - ☐ Did you look at the menu?
  - ☐ Ask if all of the staff have the proper background checks to work alone with children?
  - ☐ Review the child care provider's policy and procedures.

- Premises **[Tour Inside and the Outside of the Center]**

  - ☐ Are the classroom play areas child-friendly and safe?
  - ☐ Do you see any hazards? (cleaning chemicals, electrical cords, medications, or uncovered outlets)
  - ☐ Is the center clean?
  - ☐ Are furnishings child-sized?
  - ☐ Is the outside play area safe, clean and free from hazards?

- Programming **[Observe the Interaction betwee Staff and the Children**

  ☐ Do the children have toys and play equipment?
  ☐ Are the toys appropriate for the age of the children and safe?
  ☐ Do children play outside?
  ☐ Do young children play separately from older children?
  ☐ Are the children supervised closely by staff?
  ☐ Is there enough staff in the classrooms for the number of children?
  ☐ Do the children seem occupied by the activities?
  ☐ Does the staff seem patient with the children?
  ☐ How does the center staff communicate with the parents about issues?
  ☐ Did the center serve a snack or meal?
  ☐ What does the center do when children misbehave?
  ☐ If you were a child, would you be happy at this center?

  As a parent, your initial reaction is very important. ALWAYS TRUST YOUR JUDGMENT!

PARENTING SKILLS CHECKLIST

"If you raise your children to feel that they can accomplish any goal or task they decide upon, you will have succeeded as a parent and you will have given your children the greatest of all blessings."

-Brian Tracy

Are you using good parenting skills? Answer these easy questions and see. . .

Many people find this self-evaluation helpful to determine areas of strength or weakness in their parenting skills. Each area listed is considered to be very important in rearing healthy, happy, and successful children. A Parent's Checklist is for your personal use.

1. I am consistent, firm, and fair when I discipline my child.

2. I teach my child to identify choices and make independent decisions.

3. I know where my child is, what he or she is doing and with whom.

4. I establish family routines that include meals and study time together as well as other activities.

5. I require my child to participate in the routine chores and productive work of the family.

6. I display my child's school work on a wall, refrigerator, or bulletin board.

7. I teach my child to respect other adults and authority.

8. I make sure my child knows the rules and expectations in our household.

9. I read and respond to information sent home regarding achievement of my child.

10. I teach my child to tolerate differences in others.

11. I help my child when he or she is having difficulty in school.

12. I set an example for my child for not abusing alcohol or drugs.

13. I hug and show affection to my child daily.

14. I stress the importance of education by daily reading, checking homework, and participating in teacher conferences, open houses, and volunteering time or resources.

15. I know my child's teachers and stay in contact with them.

16. I make sure my child is in school and on time every day.

17. I set the example of hard work and personal responsibility.

18. I set aside time each day for my child to share with me what he or she has done in school.

19. I see that my child has sufficient rest and nutrition daily.

20. I take care of my child and myself through regular medical and dental care.

21. I praise my child for his/her good behavior and efforts.

22. I set a good example for my child by volunteering at my child's school and in the community.

23. I plan a family meeting once a week.

24. I encourage regular family involvement activities.

25. I understand the importance of avoiding drugs, alcohol, and other medications which the doctor feels would be unsafe during pregnancy.

26. I read with my child daily.

Research has been collaborated from:

- National Standard for Parent/Family Involvement Programs / National PTA

- No Child Left Behind Act – Parent Involvement Section 1118

- Joyce Epstein, Johns Hopkins University Center for School Family and Community Partnership

- National Coalition for Parent Involvement in Education

- The Florida Partnership for Family Involvement In Education

- Parent Resource Manual Webster's International – Judith Dato

- Hillsborough's Promise

-Hillsborough County Public Schools (Florida)

KINDERGARTEN READINESS CHECKLIST

CHILD'S NAME_______________________________________   **DATE**_______________

	MASTERED	PROGRESS SHOWN	NOT MASTERED
I. Self Help/Social Skills:			
Can use bathroom independently:	☐	☐	☐
Can dress self (button, zipper, snap, put on coat):	☐	☐	☐
Can follow two-step directions:	☐	☐	☐
Can stay on *"teacher-directed"* task for 5 minutes:	☐	☐	☐
Can follow classroom rules:	☐	☐	☐
Can appropriately express their own needs, feelings, and opinions:	☐	☐	☐
Can appropriately respond to the needs, feelings, and opinions of others:	☐	☐	☐
Has self motivation and persistence:	☐	☐	☐
Forms supportive relationships with peers and other adults:	☐	☐	☐
II. Fine/Gross Motor Skills:			
Can use proper pencil grip:	☐	☐	☐
Can use scissors correctly:	☐	☐	☐
Can use alternative feet to climb steps:	☐	☐	☐
III. Language/Literacy Skills:			
Has an understanding of the concept of the printed letter:	☐	☐	☐
Can recognize, write, and identify letters in first name:	☐	☐	☐
Can speak in complete sentences:			
Can rhyme words:	☐	☐	☐
Can handle books properly/has book awareness:	☐	☐	☐
Can identify environmental print:	☐	☐	☐
Can identify that letters make sounds:	☐	☐	☐
Can retell a story or poem/finger play:	☐	☐	☐
IV. Math/Science Skills:			
Can count 1 to 10:	☐	☐	☐
Can do one-to-one correspondence:	☐	☐	☐
Can duplicate simple patterns:	☐	☐	☐
Understands spatial relationships:	☐	☐	☐
Expands knowledge of and abilities to observe, describe and discuss the natural world, materials, living things and natural processes:	☐	☐	☐

(Circle those achieved)

Can identify basic shapes: circle, square, triangle, rectangle, other:________,________,________

Can identify colors: red, blue, yellow, green, white, black, purple, pink, brown, orange.

Can recognize numbers: 0,   1,   2,   3,   4,   5,   6,   7,   8,   9,   10.

___________________________ Date	___________________________ Date
Parent's Signature	Teacher's Signature

Developed by Luzerne County Head Start, Inc. 2002

References

Azar ST, Benjet CL, Fuhrmann GS, & Cavallero L. (1995). Child maltreatment and termination of parental rights: Can behavioral research help Solomon? Behavior Therapy, 26:599–623.

Center for Evidence-Based Practice: Young Children with Challenging Behaviors Web Site: http://www.challengingbehavior.org

Child Behavior: What Parents Can Do to Change Their Child's Behavior. Retrieved from http://www.kidschecklist.com/parenting.html

Kindergarten readiness checklist http://www.unitedwaywb.org/Kindergarten_Readiness_Checklist.pdf

Parenting Skills Checklist. Retrieved from www.sdhc.k12.fl.us/.../Parent_Family/ParentingSkillsChecklist.shtml

Parenting Style and its Correlates. Retrieved from http://www.education.com/Reference/article/Ref_Parenting

Parenting Tips for Successful Discipline- Retrieved from http://www.twu.edu/downloads/counseling/E-20_Parenting_Tips_for_Successful_Discipline.pdf

Parents are powerful role models for children: Retrieved from http://www.oh-pin.org/articles/pex-01-parents-are-powerful-role.pdf

Parent's checklist for choosing child care. Retrieved from chfs. ky.gov/NR/rdonlyres/.../O/ChildcareChecklistfor parents.doc

Six Basic Principles of Good Parenting or: What makes a good parent? Retrieved from http://www.raiseagreatkid.com/6-basic-principles-of-good-parenting.html

Ten Basic Principles of Good Parenting: There is a science to raising children. Retrieved from http://www.chiff.com/a/good-parenting.htm

Ten Practices to Avoid Parenting in Anger http://www.fshi.org/mentorscorner/FSHI-Parenting-handbook.pdf

Tips for sending kids to early childhood programs and school ready to learn Retrieved from http://www.oh-pin.org/articles/pex-11-tips-for-sending-kids-to.pdf

What research says about parent involvement in children's education in relation to academic achievement- http://www.michigan.gov/documents/Final_Parent_Involvement_Fact_Sheet_14732_7.pdf